A Fight To Fly

A Collection of Inspiring Journey's
From People With Invisible Illnesses

By: Keva Brooks Napper

A Fight To Fly: A Collection of Inspiring Journey's From People With Invisible Illnesses

For information contact: info@joycookpr.com

Book Cover by: By Way of Design, Anthony Burno
ISBN-10: 150557854X
ISBN-13: 978-1505578546
First Edition: January 2015

From the Author

The Judas Factor

What a difference a day makes? What a difference 11 years makes! How could I have imagined, from the core of my being, the birth of a nonprofit organization to help eradicate the ignorance associated with a disease that sorts to make my life a short disappearing act? How could I ever envision the pain, the heartache, the multiple joys and all the facets of a Lupus foundation? How could I, in the darkest and most difficult days, expect to be positioned such that I had to get my brain shocked to stop migraine headaches that had persisted for a month? Yes, I did say shocked! How could I even visualize having a small seizure while teaching my first grade class and be able to keep my composure without the kids knowing what was transpiring? How, as difficult as these situations were, could they be but a prelude to a more challenging recent episode? It can and it did happen to me in the last 11 years.

Recently I went for a regular visit to my dermatologist and he asked me "Do you have

Discoid Lupus only or do you have SLE (systemic lupus erythematosus)? To arrive at a conclusive answer, he decided to do a blood test and check my antibodies (ANA) to see if I really had SLE. For him to suggest this procedure threw me for a loop. I had been diagnosed with lupus (SLE) for 11 years. I also knew what I believed and prayed for. During my 11th year, I told God and no one else, that in my 12th year I was going to ask my doctor to do another test. Why my 12th year you may ask? Well I believe, like a passage in the Scriptures that depicted a woman with the issue of blood who suffered 12 long years and was made whole in the 12th year. I believed this same thing could manifest for me. Now my plan and goal had been interrupted. The doctor is saying he's testing me now! It's my 11th year and you're doing something different! My mind was running at warp speed and my emotions were running even faster and more erratic. Being stretched between hope for the best and fear for the worst, questions flooded my mind. "What if the results come back and I don't have lupus anymore?" "What if the test comes back positive and I do?" "What if the test comes back and the situation is worse?" "How do I respond?" Every cell in my body seemingly was affected, I was numb. I took the blood test and waited. Two long, nerve-racking days later the results came in my email. The normal range zone is between 0-80. My level was 1,280! Lupus was very present. I felt blindsided, as if this was my first diagnosis rather than an affirmation of what had already transpired. My public face was painted on and I went throughout the day as visibly normal as possible but every moment alone I cried. I lamented saying, "God I didn't ask for this, what am I supposed to get out of it? "God this one really hurts." "God I don't understand! Why am I having to go through the pain of this diagnosis all over again when I was just getting to the place where I could handle it?" "After all this test is a year earlier than what I wanted anyway, why now?"

I talked to a few family members and friends who prayed with me and then finally, I called my dad. His words forever changed my life. He said, "You didn't ask for the test this year and you wanted it next year. I understand your reason and the model you used from the Bible but think about this. The woman with the issue of blood in the Bible was made whole but who did she help after she was healed? Jesus had a great ministry.

He had 12 disciples at the beginning but near the end of it there was a Judas factor. You are forgetting the Judas factor. Judas committed suicide. He died early. So Jesus moved forward with the 11 that remained. The 11 that he had were able to save thousands. In your 11th year move forward and educate hundreds of people so their lives can be profitable for themselves and others. Don't become whole just to save yourself. Consider the Judas factor. How much more can you do in this 11th year with what you have? How much more powerful will your 12th year be if you consider the Judas factor and move forward? Wipe your tears and move forward. You are already healed and made whole. Help someone else by using your platform to teach them how to stand in difficult times. Teach them how to wipe the tears. Teach them how to lean on others when they are tired. Teach them how to not let the diagnosis define them. Finally, teach them how to thrive. Your test wasn't when you wanted it to be and your number didn't read what you thought it should. But when you consider the Judas factor, it places you right where you're supposed to be."

I WIPED MY FACE, HELD MY HEAD UP AND SAID,

"YES SIR."

As I'm entering my twelfth year of being diagnosed with Lupus, I know this isn't all about or just for me. I'm moving forward. I am locking arms with other thrivers to support, serve and educate the community at large to insure that this cruel mystery doesn't define us. I can't eradicate the disease that has affected 1.5 million people in the U.S. and 45,000 in my home state North Carolina. However I will help to eradicate some of the pain that it produces. I can't eradicate the fact that 1 in 250 African American women will be diagnosed with Lupus or that only 1 in 10 people diagnosed are males. Nevertheless, I can continue to teach, strengthen, encourage, enlighten and uplift those who have been affected by an invisible illness. Although we may get blindsided by things on this journey, we must always consider the Judas factor, and move forward with what we have until we become healed and whole.

Dedication

This book is dedicated to the following:

- All the lupus thrivers I have met, talked to face to face, on social media, spoken with on the phone or by email. Continue to be the warrior you are in this fight against the cruel mystery called Lupus.

- To my family for standing with me, covering me in prayer, holding me up when I wanted to fall apart, making me take my medicine when I didn't want to, making me rest when I would push too much and for simply believing in me. I don't know where I would be without the support and love of you guys.

- To the leadership and membership of Mt. Zion Baptist Church of Greensboro, Inc. You play a lead role in my story, as you have been there since the diagnosis. You've stood with me, prayed with me, supported me, encouraged me and reminded me what visible love looks like. Thank you for being a source of encouragement.

- To my nephew, Troy "TJ" Simpson Jr., a strong fighter against Prader Willi Syndrome. Rest in the arms of Jesus.

FOREWORD

The road is narrow. Its unforgiving edges leave little room for error. There are unexpected and unseen pot holes that can cause pain and despair while taking you out of alignment with the normal travel of life. No matter how you get on this road, you can find that it will take you from the mountain top of hope to the valley of depression and fear. The sharp turns of rejection or the long flat desert stretches of loneliness can make you wonder if you will ever find an oasis of relief. Just when you finally get a rest stop and get back on the road to living, you either find the road under construction or it's a dead end. So now will you stall, wreck, seek the guidance of God, find other medical help for your life or is this déjà vu?

Keva Brooks Napper, has sought out and recorded, with daily inspiration, events in the lives of fellow travelers on the road of life while dealing with Lupus and other invisible illnesses. This road, in some ways, parallels the road of the caterpillar to a butterfly and then finding it difficult to fly as designed. She helps capture the myriad facets of both defeat and victory on this journey.

As an educator and lover of life, she has always desired to help others reach their full potential in any given endeavor. Sometimes the endeavors are chosen but other times they are thrust upon us. Her overall philosophy is that "no matter where you are you can improve and make the situation better." I would paraphrase it by saying she finds a way to move;

From confined to conquest,

From tattered to tailored and

From vulnerable to victorious.

From early childhood to this very day, her warm smile and endearing personality has said I am here to help. Let her book A FIGHT TO FLY help you find a way to win your battle regardless of the intensity.

"The miracle is not always what you overcome, but what does not overcome you." – **Ryan L. Brooks**

Tabetha

In August of 2001, I was diagnosed with SLE with the anti-coagulant syndrome in addition to Lupus Nephritis in August of 2001. Before my diagnosis, I had experienced years of daily fatigue, random fevers, excruciating pain and even kidney dysfunction with no clear answers from my doctors. Yet in 2001, with a diagnosis finally in hand, I empowered myself with knowledge about this disease. I chose to be an advocate for myself and soon discovered that treating Lupus is a team effort.

I went to work every day. I refused to allow Lupus to hold me back from living. I was determined. Many days, I worked through the fatigue and reminded myself that I am stronger than Lupus. I chose to remain optimistic. Each day before work, I would read scriptures from the Bible. One of my favorite scriptures is Philippians 4:13: "I can do all things through Christ Jesus, who strengthens me." I used these scriptures as well as prayer to keep me encouraged and to shield negative energy.

In my early 30s, I faced a new battle caused by Lupus. I encountered chronic kidney failure and spent years on dialysis. In addition to scriptures and prayer, I used poetry as an outlet. Poetry allowed me an escape where I could write my thoughts and feelings freely. I found that writing calmed my Spirit and gave me a freedom to express the hurt, pain and sometimes fear that was often difficult to express verbally.

In late 2006, I had a stroke and Gran mal seizures. While in the hospital and due to complications, I became temporarily paralyzed. My family and friends were there praying for me – keeping me covered while the doctors worked on me. By the Glory of God, I awoke from my coma on Christmas Eve 2006. Though I had a long road in front me, I was comforted in knowing I had family, friends and my faith in GOD to assist me on that road to recovery.

On May 31, 2007, I was discharged from the hospital. Though I was unable to walk or talk, I was so thankful to be in my home. I would sing from my heart an old gospel song, "I don't feel no ways tired. I've come too far from where I started from. Nobody told me that road would be easy. But I don't believe He brought me this far to leave me." I continued to remember Philippians 4:13 to give me encouragement. No matter what lies ahead, I knew that by His stripes I am healed!

In 2010, I received a kidney transplant and today, my Lupus is inactive. On this journey, my faith has grown and I am spiritually stronger. I know that Lupus will not win. I understand in life that there will be strife and struggles. Nevertheless, I am blessed to know that my positive testimony can possibly help others come out of their struggles. No matter whatever else life might bring my way, I will continue to praise God.

January 2015

Sunday	Monday	Tuesday	Wednesday	Thursday	Friday	Saturday
28 Dec 2014	29	30	31	1 Jan 2015	2	3
4	5	6	7	8	9	10
11	12	13	14	15	16	17
18	19	20	21	22	23	24
25	26	27	28	29	30	31

"We do God an injustice when we place a difference between what is possible and what is impossible...because with God all things are possible." -- **Sonya D. Melton**

LaBonnie

Having an invisible illness is never easy, especially for a child. Growing up, I constantly dealt with painful joints, stomach ulcers and dealt with other unexplained illnesses. It was difficult for me to understand what was happening to me, and even easier to explain it away. I rarely admitted to my mother the problems that I was having because I did not want to be a problem. As I got older, I continued to be silent. My silence turned into a coping mechanism. It enabled me to ignore my symptoms. I learned to deal quietly with the aches and pains that I was experiencing.

While I was in high school my health issues began to manifest visibly. I had a rash over most of my body and was diagnosed with having psoriasis. The rash eventually went away with the help of topical medication. The years passed and I continued to have the same health issues that I had been having most of my life. I thought my symptoms were normal. I even was able to rationalize away the fatigue I experienced. I was an active teenager. I was involved in NJROTC. I thought my being tired was a result of participating in strenuous activities. Again, I thought my symptoms were "normal".

Things changed when my seemingly normal symptoms evolved into something greater. In 2001, I experienced unusually heavy bleeding. I visited my doctor about the issue and once he reviewed my lab results, he sent me to the emergency room. I had to be given a blood transfusion. I stayed in the hospital for a week. It was during this hospital stay that I was diagnosed with Systemic Lupus Erythematosus. In Aug of 2004 I went to the emergency room for chest pains and shortness of breath. At the time I was 6 months pregnant. The diagnosis of Lupus, being pregnant and a very low oxygen level allowed for me to be admitted. Soon after, it was discovered through chest x-rays or CT scan, that I had a few white spots on my lungs. I was given medications and told that they would like to do a biopsy. After seeing the spots on the x-ray, I prayed and asked God to remove them. I believe in miracles and believed like never before on this particular day. In the meantime, waiting on the results from a 2nd x-ray and CT scan, again I talked to God, kneeling on my knees on the cold hospital floor, expecting my miracle. When the results from the confirmation pictures came back, there were no longer spots seen on my lungs. Hallelujah!! While the doctor could not explain why there weren't any spots seen, I thanked God for the miracle. Later, the nurse was doing a routine check on my baby's heart rate when she told me that she couldn't find it. After checking a few more times and having me turn in various positions she called another nurse to examine me. After a while, it was suggested that I have an ultra sound. On August 26, 2004 my baby was pronounced dead. The nurses could not find a heartbeat because my baby, Angel's heart had stopped beating. It was never clear to me if it was because of the medication that I was given for the suspected spots on my lungs (which I did request and received drug info papers for the medication and it did mention that it could be fatal to a fetus). In emotional pain, two days later I was transferred from Women's Hospital to Wesley Long to be further evaluated for my active lupus. I stayed in the hospital a total of 21 days. I have had many more challenges since being diagnosed. I continuously keep myself educated about Lupus. I read anything that I can find to help make myself more knowledgeable about the subject. This journey has not always been easy, but with the support of family, friends and Beautiful Butterflies Inc., I know that I will continue to triumph.

February 2015

Sunday	Monday	Tuesday	Wednesday	Thursday	Friday	Saturday
1 Feb 2015	2	3	4	5	6	7
8	9	10	11	12	13	14
15	16	17	18	19	20	21
22	23	24	25	26	27	28

"No problem is strong enough to destroy me unless I believe it can." – **Edna G. Brooks** "

Zj'ya

My name is Zj'ya Westbrook, and I was diagnosed with Systemic Lupus Erythematosus (SLE) in June 2012. Once I received the news, I really didn't know what to say or think. Lupus was the last diagnosis I thought I would hear from the doctor. I knew I was sick when I started having joint pain and swelling in my hands and knees; then I started having a rash on my face that would come and go. My parents thought it was the foods I was eating and so did I, but it was lupus. I started going through my treatment at Duke Children's hospital in Durham, NC. I started taking my medication, and going through exams that were overwhelming.

I was in middle school at the time of my diagnosis and my friends would ask about my facial rash and wellbeing. I didn't want them to know that I had lupus. It wasn't any of their business. I thought about what would happen if my friends knew? How would they treat me? Would they still be my friends? I thought about that for a long time. My parents talked to me and told me it was okay to let my friends and teachers know about my disease. I didn't think it was going to turn out well, but it did. My friends treated me the same and acted like nothing was wrong with me. My parents on the other hand were hovering over me; telling me to take my medication and stay out the sun, wear my sunscreen and get some rest. I knew they were only concerned and worried about me but it still made me think about my illness more than I wanted to.

I have had lupus for 2 years now and I'm still dealing with some changes in my body. I am cool with taking my meds and going to the doctor. I don't like it, but I'm cool with it. I feel better about things today than before. Beautiful Butterflies support group helps me a lot. I didn't want to go and talk at first so I just listened to everyone else. I met some people with the same challenges and I was able to relate to what they were saying and feeling. Now I go to the support group without fear. I'm not just surviving; I'm thriving. I will overcome. I have the victory and I will live my life the way Jesus ordained it. I have adopted the saying "I may have Lupus, but Lupus doesn't have me."

March 2015

Sunday	Monday	Tuesday	Wednesday	Thursday	Friday	Saturday
1 Mar 2015	2	3	4	5	6	7
8	9	10	11	12	13	14
15	16	17	18	19	20	21
22	23	24	25	26	27	28
29	30	31	1 Apr	2	3	4

"The victory is not to change the doubter's opinion of you but to finish your assignment." – **Darnell Gray**

Denise D.

I always prided myself on maintaining good health. My family and friends will tell you that they don't ever remember me not being healthy. I'm a serious health activist. As a child, my thing was to hang out with my only brother. My parents had six girls and one boy. I was born a twin but was the middle child with my brother being two years older than me. He taught me all kinds of kid stuff. We climbed trees, played flag football, created skate boards from Christmas skates and shot marbles. I was always a child that sought out and investigated nature.

Besides physical activity there were the arts. I became a little artist all the way through junior high participating in all kinds of art shows. But then, I discovered that I was pretty articulate at voicing an opinion and had the ability to persuade others to embrace it. At that point, I ran for my first public office as the ninth grade treasurer. It was a fierce campaign but I knew I had the victory after an engaging campaign speech.

In 1971, the federal government stepped in and mandated de-segregation of the Forsyth County school system. My classmates and I were devastated as well as forced to attend high schools that were predominately white. It was then that I learned the importance of dealing with adversity.

The class of 1972 was the first to vote at the age of eighteen years of age. My twin sister Inese and I were registered to vote in the living room of our home. It was a surreal moment in time and I knew that politics and public service was what I wanted my life to be about. When I attended Morgan State University in Baltimore my passion for activism and advocacy was sealed.

I graduated with a degree in Speech Communication and returned home in 1976. I was infatuated with manufacturing all my life. Taking raw goods and making a product fascinated me and so I spent my career of 38 years doing just that. Over the years I managed and worked on several local, state and federal political campaigns. In 1990, I ran for the state house in District 67 and finished in a runoff situation that I didn't call for.

God told me not to call for the runoff because I

was going to win but not like I thought it would be. And I did. It was at that point that my life changed as I knew it. I became engulfed and engaged in anything political that would affect the quality of life of others. I was content and happy with my life. My job and community volunteerism and public service was who I was. It was who I had become.

In November 2009 I ran and won a seat on the Winston-Salem City Council. I was working two jobs more than full time. My day consisted of eighteen hours of work and six hours of sleep. For those that know me, I'm all in two hundred percent for whatever I'm doing. It was August 2012 when I started to notice the weight loss. I thought that it was due to my working out and that my efforts were finally paying off after all these years. I had no idea that there was something really wrong.

I began to feel strange and fatigue and not myself all the time. Now remember, I'd never been sick in my life. Family and friends began to comment on my weight loss but I told them it was due to my working out. By October my hair began to fall out in the back of my head. I accused my barber of giving me some type of scalp infection. I then went to my dermatologist and she prescribed an ointment for my scalp.

My sister Rita suffered from COPD and died in January 2013. By then I was very sick. I went to my doctors but nobody diagnosed any real ailment. But I continued to feel bad and lose weight. Some doctors said it was all in my head and prescribed anti-depressants that I refused to take. I knew something was wrong with me. In March, I broke out in a rash all over my chest. I went to my dermatologist and she performed a biopsy that later determined that I had lupus.

I thought okay I can live with this. At least I now know what's wrong with me. Unfortunately, that was only the beginning. Then it happened, I went to bed after a City Council meeting and literally just couldn't go anymore. My sister Tanya found me that night and called the EMTs. I thank God for Tanya finding me that night. I was rushed to the hospital and a CT scan revealed that I had a leaking appendix and a benign tumor. The surgeon removed both and after a few days I was released to go home.

The next several months were an uphill battle. After the surgery, I returned to the hospital on two other occasions for a bad case of pneumonia and inflamed cartilage that connects the lungs to the ribs. Recovery was long and painful. It was filled with a walker, being bathed by my sisters, lots of weeping, doctor visits, blood work, joint pain, muscle aches, fatigue and breathlessness. I'd never been in a place where I couldn't work out, play golf or go as I please. When I did return to work there were more days than not that I couldn't work. It was then that God spoke to my spirit and told me it was time for me to retire. I was definitely ok with that!

Through all of this I learned to be patient and wait on the Lord. I learned to allow others to help and assist me without asking. I learned the power of prayer from family, friends and strangers. I learned that even though it seemed the darkest before dawn God would bring me through. I take my life and nothing in it for granted. I laugh and cry at myself when I need to because it's not that deep. I learned that even though I have lupus – lupus doesn't have me.

April 2015

Sunday	Monday	Tuesday	Wednesday	Thursday	Friday	Saturday
29 Mar 2015	30	31	1 Apr	2	3	4
5	6	7	8	9	10	11
12	13	14	15	16	17	18
19	20	21	22	23	24	25
26	27	28	29	30	1 May	2

Keva

It started as a small patch of hair, about the size of a nickel. It puzzled me as I looked in mirror to see a raw, red spot in the back of my head for no apparent reason. Within a short amount of time the spot grew to the size of a quarter. My hair didn't shed slowly, just came out, and my scalp was completely raw. To add to it, I started getting a fever. No coughing, no sneezing, just fatigued and a fever that wouldn't break, 102, 103, for 5 days straight. My body felt like an 18 wheeler had run over it at full speed. The thought of moving or getting out of the bed made me ache. The telephone rang, it's the doctor's office. "Mrs. Napper, after reviewing all the tests and your blood work, we wanted to let you know you tested positive for Lupus." Puzzled, hurt, confused, uneducated, frightened, and tearful, I simply said, "Thank you. I'll be in to get further information and medication." I hung up the phone and cried until I went to sleep.

I spent the remainder of 2003 adjusting to medicine and learning a little about lupus but never really talked about it, not even to my family and friends. In June of 2004 there would be another episode that would get my attention concerning this fight with lupus. My dad was the senior pastor of Mount Zion Baptist Church of Greensboro Inc. at the time, and while sitting in church on a Sunday morning, his pastor, Bishop Neil C. Ellis was preaching on Generational Curses, and I began to have a Gran Mal seizure. I was in and out of consciousness and was rushed to the hospital. Before the day was over I had about four Gran Mal seizures. I ended up in ICU and woke up the next day in the afternoon. The neurologist came in and told me I had two blood clots on my brain, causing me to have a stroke. My blood pressure was fine, cholesterol was fine, and they didn't know what caused it. They later found out I had Protein S deficiency (blood disorder). Another incurable disease which they connected to lupus. After being in ICU and in the hospital for two weeks, I was able, by God's Grace, to go home needing no rehab and having no memory loss!

Six months after the stroke, I got pregnant. The doctor simply said terminate. Then he said, well these are your choices, terminate, risk the baby's life, your life, or perhaps both of your lives. Your body hasn't healed and has been through too much trauma. You should terminate while you can. Already emotionally and physically at level zero, I turned to my greatest resource, I said a simple prayer. "Lord, you handle this, because I can't." One week later I had a miscarriage.

I have had many other obstacles since my diagnosis in 2003 causing me to be a warrior in this lupus fight. All the invisible aches and pains you can't see. The swollen joints, the low white blood cell count, the chest pains that feel like a heart attack, the night my joints hurt so badly I had to crawl to the rest room in the middle of the night and pull myself up on the toilet. However, the diagnosis of the disease doesn't define who I am. I define who I am. This disease can blind side you with punches of pain and in some cases leave you feeling broken and bruised. But just as the caterpillar fights in the cocoon as it goes through the stages of molting, it never gives up until it reaches the goal of becoming a butterfly. The caterpillar could never go places the butterfly can, nor could it ever see things from the same perspective. At times when I feel like I am in this cocoon for the fight of my life, I realize the metamorphosis from caterpillar to butterfly is never easy. So as lupus and I fight within this cocoon called life, I struggle, I hurt, I am challenged but I win. If my struggle, my bruises and the broken places I've experienced help someone else while it's shaping and molding me then I'm willing to Fight to FLY!!

"To survive is to live, but to thrive is to excel." – **George W. Brooks**

May 2015

Sunday	Monday	Tuesday	Wednesday	Thursday	Friday	Saturday
26 Apr 2015	27	28	29	30	1 May	2
3	4	5	6	7	8	9
10	11	12	13	14	15	16
17	18	19	20	21	22	23
24	25	26	27	28	29	30
31	1 Jun	2	3	4	5	6

Kristi

To tell my lupus story would actually involve talking about my sorority sister Tasha Smith Dixon. My connection with lupus began in 1996, when my sorority sister and close friend Tasha said, "I have Lupus!" "What's that?" I responded. It didn't make a lot of sense because I knew nothing about that word Lupus and had actually never heard it before. But lupus was the explanation for her constant fatigue and recent joint pain.

Tasha had just gotten married a few months after her diagnosis and was told it was probably not a good idea for her to try to conceive a child. She and her husband Tyree were both only children and she desperately wanted a family. Against the doctors wishes she got pregnant. We were all concerned but Tasha was constantly saying, "As long as I see the first year of my baby's life, I'm happy!" Little TJ couldn't wait to see his mommy either and was born 3 months early on February 13, 2001. Tasha said that a birth date so close to Valentine's Day was appropriate because he was her true love! The stress of the pregnancy and childbirth was too much for Tasha's body and it lead to congestive heart failure. She received a new heart within 9 months and it seemed as if things were going well. TJ was turning 1 and the doctors' talked about releasing her in time for his birthday party which would be held on that Saturday,

February 16th. The family actually celebrated his birthday on the 13th in Tasha's hospital room and she was so delighted! She received the news that she was to be going home on the 14th, on Valentine's Day, her favorite holiday! While running several tests they discovered fluid on Tasha's lungs which needed to be removed before she could be discharged. They decided she needed surgery to remove the fluid. Tasha did not make it through the surgery and we lost her on Valentine's Day, exactly one year and one day after her baby's birth. In her own words she could be happy. I spent the next few years being angry at Lupus for taking her away. I can never enjoy Valentine's Day the same again because it reminds me of losing my sister.

Over the years, I started having tingling sensations in my hands and feet, feeling extremely cold all of the time and having an irregular menstrual cycle. I never even thought about considering Lupus as the source of my problems because these symptoms were nothing like Tasha's, but I knew something was wrong. My doctors kept saying, "Oh, yeah you're just getting older", but I knew better. Something was really wrong. Looking back, I think I can date my symptoms as far back as 2007. I experienced an episode where it felt as if an elephant was sitting on my chest. I was sweating, couldn't breathe and had a severe pain on my left side. I spent several days in the hospital and they ruled it as a mild stroke. I was only 32 years old! So from there I had more years of swelling hands and feet as well as tingling sensations in my extremities. The doctors would only contribute it to going through early menopause or stress. I changed doctors several times. In 2012, I finally got a doctor to agree that the tingling sensation and loss of color in my extremities was not normal. This was when I was diagnosed with Raynaud's Phenomenon. I accepted it as just Raynaud's until other things started happening like joint problems, severe swelling, hair loss and a lot of the other common symptoms that lead to a diagnosis of Lupus. I noticed that some days I couldn't get out of bed. I was extremely depressed and could not understand why. All of my life I have always been a go-getter. In college I carried an average of 18 to 21 credit hours a semester. I was a varsity cheerleader for the football and basketball teams, which meant I had a year round season. I was also a member of the step team for Delta Sigma Theta Sorority, Incorporated. I had always lived my life by filling my schedule with as many activities as I could, and I was able to function just fine! All of a sudden I couldn't do that anymore. That sent me into a deeper state of depression.

My mother is the one who actually thought of Lupus and downloaded the Lupus symptoms checklist from a commercial that she saw. I was able to check off all of the symptoms except for two. My doctor finally listened and referred me to see a rheumatologist. The test that the rheumatologist ran including the ANA test all pointed to systematic lupus erythematosus (SLE). I'll admit, at first I was terrified! The only information I knew about Lupus, was that it took my best friend away at an early age before she got to watch her beautiful baby boy grow up. I saw it as a death sentence. I took to social media to express what I was feeling. Talking about it seemed to help, but I didn't think anyone else knew what I was going through. Then, a friend from college and cheerleading teammate, Keva B. Napper, founder of Beautiful Butterflies, Inc. reached out to me. Through this relationship, I have learned so much about how to deal with and fight this big mystery. I now look at it as a way to force myself to take time for me. I'm a hundred percent committed to beating Lupus and being around long enough to celebrate the day they find a cure! I feel charged with not only living life for myself but also finishing the race for Tasha!

"You must accept the challenge to experience the exhilaration of victory." – **Deon Clark**

June 2015

Sunday	Monday	Tuesday	Wednesday	Thursday	Friday	Saturday
31 May 2015	1 Jun	2	3	4	5	6
7	8	9	10	11	12	13
14	15	16	17	18	19	20
21	22	23	24	25	26	27
28	29	30	1 Jul	2	3	4

"If we don't take care of ourselves and each other.....who else will?" – **Joy Cook**

Crystal

My name is Crystal and I am a survivor of SLE. I was diagnosed in 2009, but my health problems really began around 2002. I kept feeling like I had the flu. I went to doctor after doctor only to be told that I was just experiencing stress. It was easy for doctors to make that assumption because I had premature twin boys on Jan 22, 1998, and I also worked full time. This could make any woman stressed, but even though I was going through a busy life at home and work, I knew that my problems stemmed from other issues. I began to have major pain in my legs and walking was difficult. I had numbness in my hands and feet and my cognitive skills began to change. I was tested for Multiple Sclerosis at one point, but that test proved negative. I next visited a rheumatologist. I thought just maybe this doctor would be different, and that maybe he would believe that my sickness was real and not just coming from my imagination. Boy was I wrong. He had decided before I ever came into his office that I had Fibromyalgia and a B12 deficiency. He handed me a brochure and said, "I have been looking over your records and you have Fibromyalgia". He didn't even spend 15 minutes with me. The one positive thing from this office visit is that he recommended hot water physical therapy. The hot water physical therapy did seem to help manage my pain, but my fatigue was so overwhelming that I couldn't really enjoy the relief from pain that the treatment offered. I tried to schedule appointments with him many times after that hoping that maybe he might be able to provide additional services. Each time I tried, his office wouldn't schedule me because it was believed the doctor had helped me all he could and they recommended that I continue to visit my primary care physician.

Off and on over the next few years I was mainly treated for stress and pain. I went to a pain management doctor and it seemed like I was just being over medicated instead of being provided a real treatment plan to follow. One day I just decided that I wasn't going to keep taking all the strong medicine. My mind was slipping and I was really struggling to function. I suffered in silence because family members and friends all acted as if I was over emphasizing my symptoms. All I ever heard was, "you don't look sick". I had so many different symptoms that my doctor would send me to various specialists to help remedy the issues. Each doctor would treat the immediate symptom, but I would not get any substantial relief. I always kept my pain level inside because I did not want my husband or children to know just how bad I felt.

When I was finally diagnosed with Lupus in 2009, I was also diagnosed with Sjögren's Syndrome. Upon the suggestion of my eye doctor, I had a gland biopsy which resulted in the positive diagnosis. Sjögren's Syndrome (pronounced SHOW-grin's) is a chronic autoimmune disease in which a person's immune system turns against and attacks the body's own cells. In Sjögren's, white blood cells attack moisture-producing glands, such as the tear ducts and salivary glands, making it difficult for your body to produce saliva and tears. So instead of one life changing illness, my new rheumatologist diagnosed me with having SLE (Systemic Lupus Erythematosus) primary and Sjögren's secondary.

Over the years, my health issues have had a direct impact on my finances. I would have to change jobs every couple of years because my health affected my attendance and performance. My husband and I even decided to give up our home because I never knew what my job situation was going to be. The stress to maintain financial security has become a huge burden on my family. We now struggle to make ends meet which in turn causes my Lupus to flare and inevitably leads to episodes of depression. My health is finally stable enough for me to work regularly, but my salary is less than half of what it used to be. I have health insurance, but there are many times I can't afford to go to the doctor because I can't afford the copay. I know in my heart I can't complain because there are many people around the world struggling harder than I have to struggle. And, for that I am thankful. God always gets us through the hard times!

My journey with illnesses took a different turn. One year ago, I was diagnosed with Cervical Adenocarcinoma Cancer. It was diagnosed at stage 0 which is considered as pre cancer. I was advised to have a hysterectomy which was the only treatment that I ended up needing. The oncologist has recommended four pap smears this year and if everything comes back normal I can reduce my visits to two a year. I just had my third pap smear and it came back abnormal. Of course I was scared to death, but once again I found favor with God and the results came back without a trace of cancer.

Autoimmune disease is such a challenging disease. Once you are diagnosed with one disease it seems as if another disease emerges. Since my Lupus diagnosis I have battled depression, cancer, Sjögren's, psoriasis and psoriatic arthritis. I now take medicine for high blood pressure, thyroid, digestive issues, anxiety, as well as plaquenil for my Lupus. Even though plaquenil hasn't taken every symptom away, I am still able to manage much better than I did two years ago. I have hope that I can live my life with Lupus and still enjoy the great things life has to offer. Through the bad days, I always seem to find a way to manage. I have learned to compromise my schedule and participate in the activities that are most meaningful to me. I have two wonderful children that need me and I will NOT let Lupus rob them of a mother. I have Lupus, but Lupus does not have me.

July 2015

Sunday	Monday	Tuesday	Wednesday	Thursday	Friday	Saturday
28 Jun 2015	29	30	1 Jul	2	3	4
5	6	7	8	9	10	11
12	13	14	15	16	17	18
19	20	21	22	23	24	25
26	27	28	29	30	31	1 Aug

"Life is a great journey but it can only be lived one step at a time." – **Edna G. Brooks**

Rebecca

I am a 71 year old woman strong in body, mind and living a life that has always been a blessing but never easy.

My Lupus journey began when I noticed a bump on top of my head in my scalp. I remember it like it was yesterday. The bump changed daily until one bump became many. My beautician of several years advised me to see a dermatologist. I did and he suggested that I have a biopsy. He let me know that he suspected the outcome would be Lupus. The results from the biopsy confirmed the doctor's suspicion. It was Lupus. After the initial diagnosis from the first dermatologist I visited, I was referred to another dermatologist who works closely with Lupus patients and is more familiar with the disease. During my first visit with Dr. Amy McMichael, I was not sure what to expect. She performed a second biopsy and more lab work. The results were the same, Lupus.

My treatment included oral medication and special soaps and lotions for the rashes I began to develop on various parts of my body. The issues with my scalp that led to my diagnosis progressed over time. I began to feel chill sensations inside my scalp which resulted in very noticeable hair loss. Not only did I have to deal with the emotional pain of losing my hair, I also had to endure the physical pain of twenty or more injections in my scalp during a single visit to the doctor.

Sometime after my Lupus diagnosis and medical treatments, I started attending a Beautiful Butterflies support group for people affected by Lupus. In the support group, we feel we are all family. We have learned to appreciate and support one another.

My physical health has had many challenges. I have had two knee replacements. My joints always seem to hurt and I am less active than I would like to be. I live with the pain of Lupus every day but my faith keeps me going. Even still, I have my good days. There are days when the strength of the Lord washes over me. On these days, I have enough energy to spend time with my family. And, if they are lucky, they can keep up with me.

August 2015

Sunday	Monday	Tuesday	Wednesday	Thursday	Friday	Saturday
26 Jul 2015	27	28	29	30	31	1 Aug
2	3	4	5	6	7	8
9	10	11	12	13	14	15
16	17	18	19	20	21	22
23	24	25	26	27	28	29
30	31	1 Sep	2	3	4	5

Veronica

My name is Veronica Morgan Dicker. I am a 43 year old wife, mother and Nana. I was diagnosed with Lupus in 2004. My Lupus journey is exceptionally different because I also have been affected by Bullous Pemphigoid. Bullous Pemphigoid is an autoimmune disease that is characterized by tense blisters on the skin. This disease covered my body, causing me to lose 80% of my skin at one point. Needless to say it was a traumatic event. I could go further into the many terrible things that I have encountered battling Lupus and Bullous Pemphigoid, but I won't. What I will share with you is how I found peace on my journey and how I have learned to live my life with purpose.

It was not until seven years ago that I decided not to waste anymore of my time feeling sorry for myself. No more questioning God's plan, "God why me?" Life for me changed when I went to an information session. It was nothing new for me to go to these types of sessions. I would usually go and listen and leave out the same way I came in. But during this particular meeting, things were different. I went into this meeting with a changed mind, and when I left, I applied the information that I learned.

I started with a complete lifestyle change. First, I started with my mind. I began thinking better thoughts about myself and my situation. I would remind myself that I am victorious and I would encourage myself that I will live and not die. Next I began to change my diet. I learned that taking control of my diet and the things that I eat were important because the foods I eat have a direct impact on how I feel. I found that sugary, sweet unhealthy foods did not agree with my body and left me feeling sluggish and tired. I certainly don't want to add to any of my symptoms by eating poorly. If being conscious of what I am putting in my body helps me feel better, I have to make the choice to eat the right things. Finally, I began to exercise more. I use 5k walks that support Lupus as a way to motivate me to stay active. Participating in 5k walks allow me the chance to exercise while raising money and awareness for Lupus. It's a win-win.

I am using my story to help others. Sharing my story gives me a sense of purpose and fulfillment. I encourage recently diagnosed people as well as family and friends of people who have Lupus. I give them the advice that helped me: follow all of the recommendations from your rheumatologist, learn to put yourself first, eat properly, and find a support group to attend. It takes a team of support. Having support definitely makes it easier to make it from day to day.

I have been a through a great deal of pain on my Lupus journey. However I don't look at my cup as being half empty. I choose to look at it as half full. I THRIVE!

"It's not what you're in but who you're in that determines where you go in life." – **Bryan J. Pierce Sr.**

September 2015

Sunday	Monday	Tuesday	Wednesday	Thursday	Friday	Saturday
30 Aug 2015	31	1 Sep	2	3	4	5
6	7	8	9	10	11	12
13	14	15	16	17	18	19
20	21	22	23	24	25	26
27	28	29	30	1 Oct	2	3

"When you trust God, you don't have to know all the details!" – **Neil C. Ellis**

Silas

My name is Silas Pressley III, and I was diagnosed with Lupus in 2001, at the age of 17. Since my diagnoses, I have been up against many challenges such as: not being able to continue with sports, not being able to keep up with my daughter physically, and just dealing with the daily aches and pains of Lupus. Through it all, I am an overcomer.

Ever since I was a young boy, I have always been an athlete. I played football and basketball. When I got in high school, I started getting the symptoms of Lupus. After playing a full game of football on Friday nights, I would be in so much pain that some of my teammates would have to carry me off the field. The symptoms followed me to college. That is when I was diagnosed with Lupus. Due to the effects Lupus had on me physically, I had to stop playing sports all together. This was devastating because I entered college on a basketball scholarship. Within my experience with Lupus, I have learned to understand my limits, and know when to take a break or just rest. I have replaced playing sports with playing the drums for my church. I love that I have found something to do that fulfills a passion and allows me to remain active.

During my third year of Lupus, I received a wonderful gift, my daughter Ayana Aaliyah Pressley. I believe God gave her to me to help me deal with my condition. She understands my condition and does not hold it against me. She makes sure that I am well taken care of. Every time I see Ayana I forget about all of my aches and pains. She gives me a reason to keep going.

Parents who have Lupus are often challenged as to how to entertain their children. Children like to be active and play outside on sunny days. This is not always possible with Lupus. However, God blessed me with a child who understands my condition. I am thankful that God gave Ayana the gift of words. Yes, she is a jokester and we spend quality entertaining each other with laughter.

Living with Lupus is the biggest challenge I have ever had to face. I am constantly going to doctors and taking numerous pills. During the first few years of my dealing with Lupus, I went into a deep depression. God helped me overcome it by surrounding me with people who truly love me, such as my mom, grandmother and my best friend, my wife LaShanda. Having these women of God by my side makes life with Lupus much more tolerable than it would be without them.

There are moments when Lupus grabs ahold of my mind, but just before I get to a breaking point, I start praying and quoting various scriptures. Here are a few that encourage me:

"I shall not die, but live, and declare the works of the lord." **Psalm 118:17**

"Do not grieve, for the joy of the Lord is [my] strength." **Nehemiah 8:10**

"Thou wilt keep him in perfect peace, whose mind is stayed on thee: because he trusteth in thee." **Isaiah 26:3**

"...we are more than conquerors through him who loved us." **Romans 8:37**

As a young black man with lupus, I have faced and I am still facing challenges, but God has not and will not fail me. Every obstacle I have overcome helped me to become the strong man, father, and husband I am today. **I AM AN OVERCOMER, AND I AM STILL STANDING!!**

October 2015

Sunday	Monday	Tuesday	Wednesday	Thursday	Friday	Saturday
27 Sep 2015	28	29	30	1 Oct	2	3
4	5	6	7	8	9	10
11	12	13	14	15	16	17
18	19	20	21	22	23	24
25	26	27	28	29	30	31

"Pain is either devastating or motivating but you must determine which." – **George W. Brooks**

Cherokee

My name is Cherokee and I have Incomplete Lupus Erythematosus. (Yes, it is as puzzling as it sounds.) Incomplete Lupus Erythematosus is a diagnosis for patients characterized with antinuclear antibodies (ANA) and disease symptoms related to one organ system. I was diagnosed in January 2014, after unknowingly battling symptoms for years. After months of endless doctor's office visits, blood tests, procedures and prescriptions, I had come to my wits end. I could not, nor could anyone else for that matter, figure out what was plaguing me with this plethora of symptoms; rashes, migraines, nausea, vomiting, extreme fatigue, hair loss, decreased appetite, muscle weakness, joint pain, weight loss, numbness in my fingers and toes, and of course the inevitable, depression. Before my diagnosis, I lost a lot of relationships with friends because I could not hang out all night or jump up and spend all day in the sun. Even my family lost interest in my health once the symptoms were no longer new and dramatic. This was becoming a way of life for me and everyone else just kept moving along. My body didn't seem like my own anymore. I didn't recognize myself in the mirror. I no longer felt like a twenty year old, "pretty, young, thang", but more like a deteriorating seventy-five year old woman hanging on for dear life. I got tired of doctor after doctor telling me I was just depressed and stressed and it was, "manifesting physically." I desperately wanted them to understand that I was not in pain because I was depressed. I was depressed because I was in pain.

After learning my "issues" had a name, Incomplete Lupus Erythematosus, I felt a sense of lucidity followed by a shadow of uncertainty. I was happy I could prove my sanity. However, I had a long list of questions. Will it get worse? Will it get better? Was does this even mean for my life? I was not familiar with Lupus other than the fact you can't get rid of it once you have been diagnosed. I thought I would never get my life back, and that this disease would just keep progressing until I could no longer recognize myself. Well, to this day, I still do not have answers to any of these questions, but, I no longer feel that sense of ambiguity or fear. I understand that Lupus is not a predictable disease. It varies from case to case, and it goes without saying that my case is unique to me.

After starting treatment and with the support of my biggest fan and advocate, my mom, I get a little better every day. I am not afraid for the future; yes, I have my concerns, but I embrace the unknown. Through this diagnostic process, I have learned that it is quite alright not knowing what next year, next week, or even what tomorrow will bring. I can only live for today, and this is exactly what I intend to do. If I spend my days and nights worrying and sulking, I will miss out on the great opportunities right in front of me. I can worry about bills, kids, declining health and work when I am older. Now, I am twenty-one years old and I need to concern myself with this stage of my life; making healthy choices, establishing a career, and building lifelong relationships. It took a while for me to stop the pity party and start loving and appreciating myself for who I am, but now I have come to realize that I am not my disease. I have Incomplete Lupus, but it does not have me.

"Do not fear going forward slowly; fear only to stand still."
    ~Chinese Proverb

November 2015

Sunday	Monday	Tuesday	Wednesday	Thursday	Friday	Saturday
1 Nov 2015	2	3	4	5	6	7
8	9	10	11	12	13	14
15	16	17	18	19	20	21
22	23	24	25	26	27	28
29	30	1 Dec	2	3	4	5

Jamila

In 2013, between Thanksgiving and Christmas, I started experiencing pain in my left knee. I couldn't remember doing anything that would've caused the amount soreness I was feeling. As the days went on, my body started to ache in other areas, then all over. I didn't understand what was going on, what triggered it or what I could do to take the pain away. Several days went by and things did not get better, but instead progressed to the point that I wasn't able to move. It was painful to do everything from getting out of bed to lifting my arms to get dressed. I eventually went to the emergency room, and left with no answers. They said that I was possibly under stress and probably fatigued. They gave me pain pills, and told me to see my primary care doctor. When I went to visit my doctor, he too was perplexed. He believed I had rheumatic fever and referred me to a rheumatologist. Two months later after vials and vials of bloodwork, the results were in...I had an autoimmune disease known as lupus. This was diagnosis was mind boggling. There wasn't anyone in my family that had any related disorder, so I did not initially accept my diagnosis. I just knew there was a mistake, and future results would show something different. Instead, future results showed damage to my kidneys and thyroid. And from there, my journey began. I thought back to previous years where I'd experienced numerous common symptoms of Lupus that were apparently signs, although the proper testing was never done to identify what was actually going on in my body.

Lupus is indeed "the cruel mystery." The symptoms and progression are not the same for any two individuals. Therefore, the doctor can't treat any two people the same. What works for one might not work for another. I take pills daily from the time I wake up until the time I go to bed. The "right" regiment for me continues to remain a "mystery," and I was told that I may never be symptom free.

One of the most difficult parts about living with lupus is the uncertainty. I'm always worried when I go to my appointments about which organ has been affected, what new medication will be prescribed, how many times I will have to be stuck when it's time for blood to be drawn, and how much weight I've gained from the steroids that have been prescribed. The reality that it takes my body longer to heal and recover when I become ill is a constant reminder of what living with this disorder entails. I also never know how I will feel from minute to minute. Although I may feel fine one moment, I could begin to experience pain, develop a headache or become extremely fatigued in and instant. It's difficult for others to understand the rapid shift in the way I feel. It can be frustrating, discouraging and shameful when I have to tell others that I don't feel well even though I look fine and I'm smiling.

Despite all of this, I continue to live each day as I did before I was diagnosed. Of course, I'm cognizant of stressors and physical limitations, but I make plans to attend events, participate in activities, and enjoy friends and family just as I would have before I knew I had lupus. I've made the decision to not be a victim to this disease. I prayed to be a mother, and was blessed with twins. So I know this is not the end, but the beginning for me. I've learned to be strong at my weakest points. I will always be in control because having lupus doesn't mean that it has me. I am a thriver!

"The conundrum of being an inherent giver is that people take advantage of your heart, often unintentionally; but it doesn't

force you to change who you are." – **Meredeth Summers**

December 2015

Sunday	Monday	Tuesday	Wednesday	Thursday	Friday	Saturday
29 Nov 2015	30	1 Dec	2	3	4	5
6	7	8	9	10	11	12
13	14	15	16	17	18	19
20	21	22	23	24	25	26
27	28	29	30	31	1 Jan 2016	2

65

Resources and Partners

Full Time Fitness
4008 Mendenhall Oaks Pkwy
High Point, NC 27265 (336) 841-0233

Greensboro Medical Associates (rheumatology)
1511 Westover Terrace
Greensboro, NC 27408 (336) 373-0611

Wake Forest Baptist Dermatology
4618 Country Club Rd.
Winston Salem, NC 27106 (336) 716-3926

Beautiful Butterflies Inc.
A Lupus Foundation
www.mybeautifulbutterflies.com
(336) 528-4224

The S.E. L Group (social and emotional learning group) Counseling
304 W. Fisher Ave
Greensboro, NC 27401 (336) 285-7173

Cone Health Cancer Center
501 N. Elam Avenue
Greensboro, NC

Triad Health Center
2311 W. Cone Blvd
Greensboro, NC 27408
(336)288-4677

Acknowledgements

-Thanks to the amazing thrivers who contributed their stories to make this book possible! You all are awesome! I know it was difficult for some of you to be so transparent, but I'm confident that someone will be changed and enlightened by knowing that if you can fight and thrive, so can they! So THANK YOU, Tabetha, LaBonnie, Zj'ya, Denise D., Kristi, Crystal, Rebecca, Veronica, Silas, Cherokee, Jamila. You guys ROCK!!

-Thanks to those who gave their witty quotes! I appreciate you and the impartation you have poured into my life. Bishop Neil C. Ellis and Lady Patrice, Bishop George W. Brooks and Lady Edna, Pastor Bryan J. Pierce and Lady Deb, Pastor Ryan Brooks and Lady April, Pastor Darnell Gray and Lady Jichelle, Pastor Deon Clark and Lady Jen, Meredeth Summers, Joy Cook, Minister Sonya D. Melton.

-Thanks to my husband Calvin for putting up with me! Your friendship and prayers cover me at the most difficult times. Love ya! To my in-laws, Ms. Carolyn, Carlissa, Troy, Kyuanna and the Napper

Family, thanks for the love!

-Thanks to my parents for not only giving birth to me, but helping me birth this vision. You continuously encourage me, walk with me through this fight, pray with me, go with me to the doctor, hold me up when the reports aren't good, you've picked me up off the floor when I've totally lost it, and believed in me enough to support everything I spoke, not just with your physical presence but with your financial support. None of this could exist without you. I'm forever indebted for your agape love.

-Thanks to my brother Kevin and sis Kim, my nieces and nephews; Jocelyn, Kiandra, Keyon, Gavin, Kaleb for being there since day one, and always making me laugh! Our family trips are THE BEST!! To my cousin siblings LOL! Kendra, Tasha, and Derrick, thanks for consistently being there through thick and thin. You too Alyce! ☺ Thanks Kennedy W., Joi and JJ Jeter.

-Thanks to my best friend Sonya Melton for all your hard work on this project. From the concept to the writing you were there. Forever friends! Thanks girl!!

-Thanks to Dominique, Diatra, Kierre and Monica W., for being my road buddies, going with me on speaking engagements, telling me to "tighten up," and making sure I never went anywhere without having a good laugh!!

-Thanks to the Board Members of Beautiful Butterflies Inc., the Team Members, and all the volunteers. You all work tirelessly and I appreciate being able to work with you and call you family!

-Thanks to the best publicist ever, Joy Cook PR! It was definitely a God connection when we met and I'm so grateful that I can call you boss, friend and sister. Thanks for being who you are and the amazing business partner that you are. I'm grateful and excited about where we are going!

-Thanks to Kimberly K. Moorman for understanding and working with me when I had a head full of hair and when I didn't. You walked with me during the process and even now you make sure my scars aren't noticeable. Thank you for helping me maintain healthy hair even when Lupus fought hard against it.

-Thanks to Nancy McLean, Rev. Odell Cleveland, Mae Douglas and Tamera Ziglar for your wisdom and guidance that helped to push me out of the nest.

-Thanks to Damion Mills for your support.

-Thanks to Bishop Sheldon and Co-Pastor Joyce McCarter for your prayers and support.

Made in the USA
Middletown, DE
25 June 2016